What Our Readers Have Said...

Applicability

"These books are great tools that should be used as guidelines for our everyday supervisory practices. You need to take the time to do a short self-evaluation when reading them."

•

"The Pinpoint Training Series delivers information that could be used in a lot different areas."

•

"The things and problems we deal with everyday are discussed in these books."

Convenience

"I like this because I can take them with me to read at a convenient time. I feel the little time I have to spend in the office is best use on activities that directly relate to revenue opportunities. I like the short amount of time it takes to keep up with these."

•

"I prefer the self-study approach; it fits in with my schedule."

•

"I like the fact that the format allows the books to be reviewed as time permits. All work has been conducted on personal, evening/weekend time."

•

"Easy to use... if you put the time into it."

Challenge

"My thought is that the real value of these books comes into effect when doing the action plans."

•

"I like the fact that the format allows assignments to be reviewed as time permits."

Clarity

"Short and sweet. These books are easy to comprehend."

•

"Easy to use, understand, and reference if needed."

Relevance

"I have enjoyed reading these books. They are relevant to today's work environment and the ongoing change in the way we manage our workforce."

•

"I believe the contents of the Pinpoint series are excellent. It causes one to reflect on the daily dynamics in working with oneself as well as with management and peers."

Boosting Team Communication

Pinpoint Leadership Skill Development Training Series

TIMOTHY F. BEDNARZ

MAJORIUM
BUSINESS PRESS

Pinpoint Leadership Skill Development Training Series
"Boosting Team Communication"
Timothy F. Bednarz

Graphic design: Monika Pawlak

Majorium Business Press
2025 Main Street
Stevens Point, WI 54481
715.342.1018 • 800.654.4935

ISBN 978-1-882181-79-7

Printed in the United States of America

Introduction

The Pinpoint Leadership Skill Development Training Series is designed for targeted training and education regarding increased improvement in a specific skill or competency.

Each book within this series is designed to be easy to use, understand and apply to your job. It can be used as a basis for training individuals, as a discussion guide or as a personal training tool.

Each chapter within this book discusses a specific concept. When you have completed all eight chapters you should have a 360º perspective of the topic.

Additionally, each chapter is divided into specific sections:

- The first section provides you with an overview of the topic
- The Implications section discusses why the concept is important, and why it is important to learn and apply.
- The Strategies, Tips & Techniques to Apply section teaches how to use and apply the particular concept to your work.
- The Points to Ponder section gives you something to think about or to be discussed with a group setting. These are questions not meant to be immediately answered, but to be pondered over time.
- The Training Activity section provides you with the tools to transfer what you have learned to your job. It is designed to help create an action plan to effectively apply the concept.

Each of the topics in this series is time-tested and proven in the marketplace. They have been used by thousands of employees as training tools. Many of the users have commented that what made these books valuable, was the ability to refer to them when a problem surfaced. They indicated that they remembered reading about the exact problem. They referred back to these books and found an appropriate solution.

You will find them equally valuable as a resource in your professional development library.

Table of Contents

LEARNING OBJECTIVES:

- To identify the critical factors and benefits of communication principles and practices and the impact they have upon teams.
- To understand the implications and ramifications that either enhance, or diminish a team's communication process.
- How to overcome the problems and pitfalls associated with improper communication practices.
- How to apply effective strategies to enhance team communication.
- How communication impacts the decisions a team makes.
- To identify the expected results and outcomes of a team's effective use of communication techniques.

1

Creating Open Lines of Team Communication

The ability of individuals to openly communicate with one another in the team environment is essential to the successful development of teams. This is because teams must be able to discuss and reconcile their conflicting points of view and opinions. This process is essential to effective problem solving and decision making. Consequently, good open communication techniques are required in order for teams to be effective.

IMPLICATIONS — WHAT THIS MEANS TO YOU

Before teams can be effective, members must learn to work together. And before members can work together, they must learn how to communicate. Quite often problems in both the work and team environments are the result of poor communication between individuals. One of the key benefits of employing a team structure for problem solving and decision making is that it forces individuals to work within a structured framework, compelling them to communicate effectively with one another.

This is important for leaders to understand because a team's framework boundaries and structures not only define how it operates and communicates. Open effective communication requires framework boundaries and structures that compel employees to communicate effectively. While this may seem awkward initially, once team members become familiar with the structure and framework of open communications, both time and effort will be reduced as communications improve.

STRATEGIES, TIPS & TECHNIQUES TO APPLY

Specific behaviors define open communications within the team environment. It is essential that all team members are encouraged to use effective communication skills and practices that make discussions and meetings more effective. The following are ideal communication behaviors that should be encouraged and exhibited by team members.

Initiate Discussions

Communication requires a free-flow of ideas, input and feedback. Team members must be encouraged to openly initiate discussions within the team environment. In doing so, they stimulate creative thinking in themselves and others.

Seek Information

Team members should openly seek information as well as the opinions of their colleagues. In their efforts to seek outside sources of information, individuals should actively refer to available documentation and data. It is important that teams build decisions and solutions upon objective facts and avoid subjective inference that only leads to potential problems.

Suggest Alternatives

Team members need to suggest procedures and alternatives for reaching goals and objectives. This stimulates discussion and creative thinking regarding how to solve a problem and arrive at a consensus.

Clarify Ideas

Ideally, team members should learn how to clarify or elaborate upon their ideas. Not only does an elaboration of ideas using brainstorming techniques help explain an individual's thinking, but it also often allows one concept to build upon another and thus stimulate the thinking of others.

Summarize Position

Throughout the team process, it is important for team members to periodically stop and summarize the position that the team is currently in. This consolidates the team's thinking, clarifies all of the issues discussed to date, and allows the team to arrive at a consensus before moving ahead.

Test Consensus

As teams progress through their decision making and problem solving processes, it is important not only to summarize, as discussed in the previous point, but also to regularly test for consensus within the group. This maintains a smooth flow for the team and prevents individuals or groups from biasing the decision making process through their personal agendas.

In addition to using these specific concepts to facilitate open communication in the team environment, individual team members must act as gatekeepers for the entire group. They must be attuned to the flow of the discussion and direct conversational traffic. Their responsibilities include throttling down dominant talkers, avoiding simultaneous conversations, and making room for reserved individuals who are reluctant to offer their feedback and suggestions. They must also keep the conversation focused and on track. Most importantly, open communication requires that team members practice appropriate manners and courtesy within the group environment. Common courtesy and appropriate behavior can go a long way toward maintaining a free and open discussion.

POINTS TO PONDER – SOMETHING TO THINK ABOUT

1. During discussions and conversations, do you seek information, refer to facts and data, and seek the opinions and viewpoints of others?
2. How often do you test for consensus within your team to make sure that everyone agrees with the actions being taken?

TRAINING ACTIVITY – APPLICATION & ACTION PLAN

1. Practice the role of gatekeeper in both formal and informal discussion settings. Whether during a formal business meeting or at a gathering of friends and associates, make an attempt to monitor and direct the conversational traffic by doing the following:
    a. Control dominant talkers.
    b. Make room for shy and reserved individuals.
    c. Elicit specific input from individuals who have not interacted in this conversation.
    d. Avoid simultaneous conversations.
    e. Keep the discussion focused, and prevent digression from the topic.
2. Continually practice these skills until you recognize what occurs in an active conversation and discussion.

2

Good Team Communication – the Vehicle to Understanding

Within the team environment, facts, data and information must build a solid foundation for members to create innovative solutions and effective decisions where open dialogue is both encouraged and welcomed. Only when diverse viewpoints and perceptions are taken into account can effective and productive decisions be made.

IMPLICATIONS – WHAT THIS MEANS TO YOU

Many individuals have taken their cue from the popular media when it comes to discussions: they are vocal, animated and often intolerant of differing opinions. This style of dialogue appears to be biasing many forms of open communication. While this form of communication is fast-paced and often interesting, it is not appropriate in a team environment. Teams must learn how to openly communicate about all aspects of conflict and problems that they have to deal with. Loud and animated discussions are not only inappropriate, but also often waste time and are unproductive.

It is important for leaders to understand that the form of communication often seen in the media fails to take into account many of the facts relevant to a discussion. In the team environment it is dangerous for leaders to allow members to easily dispose of facts and replace them with opinions and perceptions. It is important for leaders and team members alike to deal with data that make decision making and problem solving more effective and productive. Leaders that allow team members to succumb to subjective opinions and perceptions will find that the team quickly collapses and becomes unproductive.

STRATEGIES, TIPS & TECHNIQUES TO APPLY

One of the critical factors that affect open communication lies in the use of statements of fact versus statements of inference. The differences between the two are readily observable.

Statements of Fact

- Can only be made after direct observations.
- Are limited by observation.
- Are limited by number.
- Lead to an agreement.

Statements of Inference

- Can be made at any time.
- Go beyond observation and often do not even require any observation of fact.
- Are not limited.
- Lead to disagreement.

It is important for team members to understand the difference between fact and inference. When team members ignore or overlook facts and deal only with inference, they tend to jump to conclusions, which then leads to faulty decisions and solutions. A common problem in open communication is that many people really do not know what they are talking about and are rarely challenged within the team environment.

Most problems do not lend themselves to factual observation and, therefore, problems are exacerbated on the inference level. Many individuals make the mistake of treating inferences as fact. They tend to repeat what they hear without bothering to verify the information, and then presume to have knowledge, when all they have is opinions.

Leaders must distinguish between statements of fact and statements of inference. They can do this by asking themselves a simple question before making a statement: "How do I know this?" Then, when participating in a discussion, leaders should ask team members, "How do you know this?" This is not meant as a challenge or an affront to the other individual, but as a method of determining whether the statement is factual. Based upon that information, leaders and the other participants within the discussion group can make a qualified decision on whether or not to accept the statement as factual. It will not always change the discussion or outcome, but is nevertheless an important distinction to make.

POINTS TO PONDER — SOMETHING TO THINK ABOUT

1. Do you readily accept what team members say as a statement of fact without accurately questioning the validity of their assertion?
2. How many decisions have you made based upon what you thought were facts when they were in fact statements of inference or opinion?

TRAINING ACTIVITY — APPLICATION & ACTION PLAN

1. On a sheet of paper create three columns and entitle them, "statement," "fact" and "inference."
2. Over the next several days, make a habit of taking notes during various meetings and listing the various statements made.

3. List each statement on the sheet of paper.
4. Categorize the statement as either one of fact or of inference.
5. Determine the basis upon which you have made this decision by identifying the fact behind the statement or the explanation of the opinion.

3

A Team's Credibility Rests on Its Communication Ability

Within the team environment, communication between members is structured and actively monitored in a manner that allows and encourages conflict to be fostered and discussed, creating positive solutions to complex problems.

IMPLICATIONS – WHAT THIS MEANS TO YOU

It is essential that leaders utilize both structural and interactive components to manage the integrity of the team. Most teams must deal with issues and concerns that can result in conflict among personal agendas and internal political conflict. The structure and integrity of the team enables open communication that does not bias interaction between team members nor favor any specific perspective or viewpoint.

A leader implementing a structure of integrity to avoid bias and intimidation allows open discussion and communication between team members and fosters an atmosphere in which creative solutions can be considered and discussed. Consequently, a consensus can be arrived at in a productive and efficient manner.

STRATEGIES, TIPS & TECHNIQUES TO APPLY

Open communication within a team environment is fostered and sustained using both structural and interactive elements that monitor and control communications throughout the entire process.

Structural Controls

In its formative stages, team communication is defined by the tasks assigned by the team charter. Teams are structured according to the framework, norms and boundaries developed through team consensus. These elements provide team members with the parameters for conflict and communication. In other words, the team structure gives members the guidance and direction they require to deal with conflict and productively brainstorm solutions. It should be noted that communication breakdowns occur when leaders and facilitators fail to actively and fairly enforce the criteria established by the team members in the formative stages.

Interactive Elements

The two primary team roles that contribute to open communication within the team environment are the team leader and facilitator. Both roles complement and support each other in the implementation of open team communication and conflict resolution.

The team leader sets the agenda for members and monitors their meetings. He or she provides the criteria and directs the business of each meeting. During open meetings, the team leader acts as an observer, withholding his or her opinions, perceptions and feedback, and only gets involved to keep the team members focused and on course.

The team facilitator plays a more active role in the team process, keeping members on target to ensure that they address issues and to provide for periods of team maintenance. It is the team facilitator's duty to maintain the process of the team and direct the manner in which the discussion is conducted. Additionally, the team facilitator is responsible for being aware of how members feel in response to the issues being discussed. In this capacity, team facilitators are continually seeking feedback and ensuring that all team members are actively involved in the discussion.

Both the team leader and facilitator are responsible for maintaining the structural integrity of the team, ensuring that it remains on task and that its norms, framework and boundaries are continuously respected. In this manner, conflict can be fostered within the environment without polarizing team members according to personal beliefs. When leaders and facilitators threaten the integrity of the team by allowing personal agendas and viewpoints to dominate, the ensuing conflict can destroy its structure, rendering efforts ineffective and unproductive.

POINTS TO PONDER – SOMETHING TO THINK ABOUT

1. Do you agree that conflict can be handled more smoothly within a structured environment?
2. Do you feel that communication is enhanced or inhibited in a structured team environment?

TRAINING ACTIVITY – APPLICATION & ACTION PLAN

1. Identify how the following elements can facilitate open communication within your team structure.
    - Norms
    - Tasks
    - Framework
    - Boundaries
2. Identify the specific components of each element that facilitate open communication.

3. Identify how these components can be used to actually bring about open communication.
4. Determine the barriers in these components that can inhibit or diminish communication.
5. Determine how the barriers can be removed.

4

Overcoming Common Communication Problems

As teams are composed of different personalities with different communication styles, communication problems will occur even when team structures are properly constructed and implemented.

IMPLICATIONS — WHAT THIS MEANS TO YOU

Leaders must learn to deal with the practical elements of communication and overcome problems associated with group or team dynamics before moving ahead with more advanced communication issues.

It is important for leaders to understand that before teams can learn to communicate effectively, team members must first learn to communicate by each respecting what the other has to say. Leaders will find that this is the initial challenge that must be overcome after team formation.

STRATEGIES, TIPS & TECHNIQUES TO APPLY

Leaders should understand the common problems experienced by groups that can hinder the effectiveness and productivity of the team.

Floundering

Teams commonly have trouble initiating and ending discussions. Members flounder, wondering what actions to take next. Resistance is experienced as the team moves from one phase of the discussion to the next.

Problems from the onset suggest the team lacks clarity or is overwhelmed by the assignment. These startup problems suggest that team members are not comfortable enough with one another to engage in meaningful discussions.

Floundering during discussions suggests that the team has not arrived at a consensus. Team members can be reluctant to expose their work to review and criticism.

Overbearing Participants

Overbearing participants wield a disproportionate amount of influence over the team. They often have a senior rank within the company or possess in-depth technical knowledge. While most teams benefit from their participation, they can cause problems when they forbid any discussion that encroaches on their area of expertise or authority. Overbearing participants will tend to see such group solutions as unworkable, or they will use technical jargon signaling that the subject is off-limits to the group.

Leaders can minimize these problems by reinforcing to the team that, as long as it pertains to the current subject, no area is off-limits. Privately, leaders can talk with overbearing individuals to let them know that it is important for the group to explore the particular subject and for individuals to understand the process.

Dominating Participants

Some team members can consume a disproportionate amount of time by talking too much. Their excessive input inhibits other members of the team from participating. Leaders should structure discussions to encourage equal participation, and openly solicit input and contributions from all team members.

Reluctant Participants

Reluctant participants may feel shy or unsure of themselves in the team, and must be encouraged to contribute their ideas and perspectives. Problems can develop when there are no activities built-in to persuade these individuals to participate.

Leaders must act as gatekeepers to the discussion by openly and actively soliciting input and contributions from these individuals. These measures ensure balanced participation from the entire team.

Self-Assured Statements

Some individuals express personal beliefs and assumptions in a self-assured manner. These statements are so forceful that other team members assume they are hearing a presentation of facts. Consequently, members are reluctant to question these statements without facts and data to defend their position. They may also fear being wrong and thus losing face with the team.

Leaders cannot allow unquestioned acceptance of opinions as facts. They must use techniques and questions that compel members to support their statement with facts and to hold it up to the scrutiny of the entire team.

Rush to Accomplishment

Many teams will have individual members who are impatient and wish to rush through the training activity. These members will come to a decision before the team has had the time to discuss and consider alternative solutions. They will then urge the group to decide matters quickly, and will discourage any further efforts to analyze or discuss the matter. These members can communicate their impatience using nonverbal behavior or direct statements.

Leaders must remind the group of their focus and make sure that specific members do not exert pressure on the team to finish prematurely. If all else fails, leaders may need to directly confront the offender.

Attribution

As a way of bringing meaning to apparent disorder and confusion, people tend to attribute motives to individuals they disagree with or don't understand. This behavior can lead to hostility in the team environment. Leaders must reaffirm the purpose, boundaries and framework of the training exercise and intervene when such behaviors are exhibited by team members.

Discounting

Discounting occurs when team members fail to assign other members' ideas and options any validity, credence or credit. If discounting happens frequently, teams can experience hostility.

Every team member deserves respect and attention from the entire team. Leaders must ensure that the team is trained from the onset in active listening and other constructive behaviors. When possible, the leader should provide support to the discounted individual. Leaders will also need to privately discuss the matter with the team member who is responsible for discounting.

Digression and Tangents

Wide-ranging and unfocused team discussions are a natural tendency as teams stray from the topic. While some digressions may be entertaining, they divert the team from the purpose of the activity. Team facilitators are responsible for bringing these discussions back to the team's agenda.

Feuding Team Members

Feuding team members can disrupt the entire team with their personal disagreements. Usually these feuds predate the team and are best dealt with outside of the team environment. Leaders can offer to facilitate a discussion to end the personal feud or at least arrive at an agreement concerning their behavior in the team setting.

POINTS TO PONDER – SOMETHING TO THINK ABOUT

1. What are the biggest communication obstacles facing your team?
2. Do you see one or two dominant personalities causing the majority of team problems?

TRAINING ACTIVITY – APPLICATION & ACTION PLAN

1. Review the problems listed below and identify those experienced by your team.
    - Floundering
    - Overbearing Participants
    - Dominating Participants
    - Reluctant Participants
    - Self-Assured Statements
    - Rush to Accomplishment
    - Attribution
    - Discounting
    - Digression and Tangents
    - Feuding Team Members
2. Identify the specific problems and the individuals responsible.
3. Determine the strategies that should be employed to eliminate these problems.
4. Implement the strategies.

5

Handling Disruptive Situations and Individuals

Within many workplace environments, leaders will find themselves in the role of team facilitator. In this capacity, leaders must direct and control team meetings and discussions in order to allow for the free-flow of ideas by all members of the team.

IMPLICATIONS — WHAT THIS MEANS TO YOU

Within the team environment, leaders are dealing with a group of individuals who each has a personal agenda, bias and perspective. In many circumstances, leaders can effectively mold these individuals into a working team. In others, one or more members can stoutly resist the work of the team. These members may not agree with the purpose of the team or feel it threatens their personal position. Unfortunately, these individuals can be disruptive enough to prevent the team from functioning, frustrating leaders and members alike.

Leaders should understand that when individuals are given the opportunity to openly participate and make their views known, some will actively work against the leader and the progress of the team. As these individuals can be devious or openly hostile, it is essential that leaders recognize their behaviors for what they are. Once done there are specific actions leaders can take to handle these individuals or motivate the team to police themselves.

STRATEGIES, TIPS & TECHNIQUES TO APPLY

Due to the nature of group dynamics, leaders should anticipate and be prepared for the fact that an individual's behavior might occasionally disrupt team discussions.

Anticipate and Prevent

When individuals organize into effective teams, most problems can be anticipated and prevented. This happens as members spend time getting to know each other, establishing ground rules and agreeing to norms of group behavior.

Group Problem

Many problems arise because individual team members allow or even encourage them in some manner. Leaders should examine each problem in light of what the team allows and encourages, and what it can do to facilitate more constructive behavior.

Control Reactions

Teams can exhibit a variety of behaviors: some minor occurrences that don't inhibit team discussion and progress, others highly disruptive and even chronic.

Leaders must respond appropriately to the seriousness of the problem, ignoring fleeting disruptions while directly confronting chronic or seriously disruptive behaviors. Experienced leaders as facilitators develop a range of responses to typical problems.

Non-Intervention

There are times when leaders need not intervene, as individual team members will handle the offending behavior themselves. In this case leaders should be available to guide and direct discussions provoked when one member confronts another.

Minimal Intervention

Leaders can discuss the problem or situation outside of the group environment with disruptive team members. Constructive feedback should be given and solutions agreed to.

Impersonal Group Time

Leaders can discuss the problem with the entire team prior to their meeting in order to focus their attention on how they encourage the problem and what they can do differently to discourage it. The problem should be treated as a team issue, with discussions of personalities and personality issues avoided.

Personal Confrontation

When other attempts have failed to rectify the offending behaviors in the team setting, leaders must become more assertive with the responsible parties. Direct action can be taken by the leader to remedy the situation.

Group Intervention

As a last resort and when all other approaches have failed, leaders may need to deal with offending behaviors in the presence of the team. In such an instance they expose the member(s) responsible for the offending behaviors to the open critique of the team.

This technique must be used sparingly, with leaders anticipating reactions and responses in order to minimize the hostility and defensiveness of offending team members.

POINTS TO PONDER — SOMETHING TO THINK ABOUT

1. How have you dealt with disruptive individuals and behaviors in the past?
2. Have you been intimidated by disruptive individuals?

TRAINING ACTIVITY – APPLICATION & ACTION PLAN

1. Review team or group situations that you have been involved in.
2. Identify ways individuals have disrupted the team environment.
3. Separate disruptive behaviors into two categories: "open" and "devious."
4. List the characteristics defining each of these behaviors.
5. Determine how these lessons can be applied in the future.

6

Breakdowns of Communication

Since leaders are dealing with individual personalities in the team environment, it is unrealistic to expect that communication will never break down. Even within the most effective and efficient team environment, issues and situations will arise that will cause an entire breakdown of team communication.

IMPLICATIONS – WHAT THIS MEANS TO YOU

The breakdown of communication in the team environment often occurs when trust and respect are diminished or ignored by individual team members. Breakdowns also occur when chronic conflict has not been resolved within the team. Another source of communication breakdown is when team members feel their personal interests are stronger than the needs and identity of the team. These individuals are motivated by their personal desires and will do anything to achieve them, including disrupting the team environment.

It is important for leaders to recognize that communication breakdowns will occur within the team environment. In the early stages of team growth, communication problems and breakdowns are more frequent, as individuals struggle to obtain position and retain power in a new and changing environment. However, in more mature and structured teams, leaders will find that the team itself will deal with the communication problem according to its defined boundaries, rules and standards.

Leaders should be aware that a breakdown in communication can have long-term ramifications on the structure and effectiveness of the team. Therefore, it is important for them to recognize potential problems and the symptoms in order to anticipate issues, such as those discussed below, before they occur.

Loss of Trust and Respect

If leaders allow problems to fester and lead to a breakdown of team communication, they will experience a corresponding breakdown of trust and respect among team members that can be difficult, if not impossible, to restore. These circumstances can be fatal to the team and might require the formation of a new team in order to overcome them. Broken trust requires prolonged periods of time to be reestablished. Leaders need to be aware of this and take appropriate action to reduce the occurrence of chronic problems that can result in the loss of trust and respect among team members.

Hindered Free-Flow of Ideas

Once communication has broken down among team members, leaders will observe that discussions become more emotional and subjective rather than objective and factual. When discussions are based on emotion rather than fact, brainstorming will diminish to the point that there is no free-flow of ideas among team members. This effectively halts the team process until the issues causing the breakdowns are dealt with.

Intimidation

Leaders who experience a breakdown of communication observe that certain members will attempt to take control of the team process, subjugating the team to their personal agendas and perspectives. Once done, these individuals will use emotional responses to intimidate other team members into accepting their points of view. This is where the bonds of trust and respect among team members can be broken. The communication breakdown destroys the team structure and subjects it to the will of one or more members.

Bias

Once the breakdown of communication has led to the destruction of the team order by one or more team members, a specific bias is created that supports the personal agendas of these individuals. When members allow the team process to be subverted by particular individuals, they undermine the entire team effort.

Faulty Decision Making

The breakdown of communication in the team environment inevitably leads to faulty decision making. Specific biases that hinder the free-flow of ideas prevent teams from considering all options and alternatives when making decisions. Consequently, decisions are impacted by the biases of the specific individuals controlling the team. In these circumstances, decision making and outcomes will be flawed.

Individuals who have hijacked the team process will use the team environment as a cover to mask their activities when decisions produce faulty results. As they do not want to be held accountable for their behaviors and actions, they will place blame for the decision on the team environment.

POINTS TO PONDER – SOMETHING TO THINK ABOUT

1. Have you experienced a communication breakdown within your organization?
2. Have you observed how undercurrents and political agendas within your organization cause these breakdowns?

TRAINING ACTIVITY – APPLICATION & ACTION PLAN

1. Based upon personal experiences, determine how breakdowns in communication have occurred within your organization.

2. Think of situations where specific breakdowns in communication have occurred.
3. Determine why the breakdowns in communication occurred.
4. Who was responsible for them?
5. Recall what happened when communication finally broke down.
6. Determine the consequences and results.
7. Identify the final outcome resulting from the breakdowns in communication.
8. Identify the specific lessons that you have learned from analyzing each of these steps.

7

Communicating the Way to Better Team Decisions

One of the primary reasons organizations and companies go through the effort of developing a qualified team environment is to produce better decision making that results in more positive outcomes. This creates a more effective, efficient and productive work environment that helps ensure the success of the organization.

IMPLICATIONS — WHAT THIS MEANS TO YOU

Good decision making is facilitated by open and effective team communication that allows teams to consider all perspectives and points of view. The synergy of the team allows it to make decisions and outcomes that individuals alone would be unable to reach. Properly done and implemented, effective team decision making makes the job immensely easier for everyone involved.

When leaders build an effective team structure and facilitate its activities, they will find that teams are more effective and productive at making decisions than leaders alone would be. This not only makes the leader's job easier, but also enables their organizational unit to be more effective in implementing new decisions.

STRATEGIES, TIPS & TECHNIQUES TO APPLY

The structure and synergy created in the team environment greatly enhances decision making in all organizational settings. This section discusses what contributes to this enhanced decision making ability.

Increased Informational Flow

The structure and makeup of teams typically allows them to develop more information and data than the average individual is capable of producing. Additionally, because of the number and combination of individuals, teams can analyze information and data more effectively and efficiently than a single individual. These enhanced analytical skills allow teams to base their decisions more on facts and data in order to support their conclusions and recommendations.

Balanced Perspectives

The structure of the team allows for the input of more feedback and perspectives on any specific issue or topic because all team members are mandated to participate and supply their feedback. The team has the ability to produce a balanced perspective on any issue it reviews.

All Points of View Considered

The brainstorming and consensus-building techniques employed by most teams allow them to consider all points of view and perspectives supplied by team members. Throughout the process, concepts are built upon in order to consolidate ideas and perspectives and use the synergy of the group to create more powerful solutions. This allows the team to weigh alternative solutions before reaching a final decision.

Solutions Prioritized

The consensus building and synergy of the team in the decision making mode allows it to consider, weigh and prioritize all possible solutions to any issue or problem. This process is based on criteria established by the team ahead of time, freeing it from any personal bias or agenda. It allows teams to effectively filter all potential solutions in order to arrive at the best possible decision.

Positive Outcomes

The team process allows people to thoroughly consider all points of view and create balanced solutions that ultimately produce positive outcomes for the organization.

It should be noted that initial decision making in new team environments can be awkward and time-consuming. As teams become more experienced and mature in making decisions, the entire process will become more streamlined, automatic and efficient. Leaders should avoid the temptation of minimizing the team's ability to grow, especially during the early stages of team development. Doing so will hinder its potential for growth, effectiveness and productivity.

POINTS TO PONDER – SOMETHING TO THINK ABOUT

1. Do you feel decision making is enhanced within the team environment, or do you feel that you can make better decisions on your own?
2. Where do you feel that team decision making really impacts your organization?

TRAINING ACTIVITY – APPLICATION & ACTION PLAN

1. Recall a problem or issue that a team solved based on solid team principles.
2. Identify the solution that you as an individual leader would have made

regarding this problem or issue.

3. Identify the solution or decision made by the team.
4. Compare and contrast your decision with the team's decision.
5. Analyze the depth and thinking of your decision versus that of the team's decision.
6. Compare and contrast the conclusions that you arrived at versus the conclusions the team arrived at.
7. Identify the lessons to be learned from this analysis.

8

Improving Team Communication — a Never-Ending Process

One of the key benefits of a maturing and developing team is to be found in the enhancement of communication throughout the team process. The results are improved information, knowledge and expertise flowing through the organization with better overall decisions and outcomes.

IMPLICATIONS — WHAT THIS MEANS TO YOU

As teams grow and become more effective, one of the key elements contributing to a foundation of open communication within the team environment is the development of strong personal relationships between members. As they learn to trust each other, members become more respectful and collaborative in their efforts, work, and communication of key information. The previous competitive environment in which individuals were both suspicious and partisan in their viewpoints and personal agendas is ultimately removed, reducing the barriers to open team communication.

Leaders understand that once a respectful and trusting team environment is developed, communication and the work of the team are enhanced. This improvement allows teams to tackle more complex and controversial topics, issues and concerns. Any conflict that results from these situations is viewed as natural and helpful in the resolution of issues and problems. An effective and mature team is able to focus on issues while ignoring the personalities and personal agendas of individual members. Once teams have achieved this status, their ability to work effectively is greatly enhanced, increasing their overall productivity and efficiency.

STRATEGIES, TIPS & TECHNIQUES TO APPLY

As individual team members learn to work together and cooperate in an open and non-threatening atmosphere, and as they establish personal levels of trust and respect among team members, the barriers to open communication are effectively removed. This results in measurable benefits for the organization.

Free-Flow of Information

One of the strongest benefits of open communication within a team environment, and within the organization as a whole, is the increased and enhanced free-flow of information. As teams mature, develop and learn to work effectively with one another, many barriers to open communication are eliminated. The fewer the barriers, the more freely information flows throughout the organization, which leads to a more open and honest sharing of information and an elimination of incomplete and mixed messages that were used by individual members to establish their power base.

Information flows freely up, down and throughout the organization. Free-flow of information enhances decision making because teams have better data and expertise to base their critical decisions upon. More effective decisions can then be made by consensus to efficiently use the resources available to the organization and fully commit the team to implementation.

Creativity

As teams mature and develop, a certain synergy is created within the organization. As information flows freely throughout the organization and relationships are more firmly established in an open and non-threatening atmosphere, individual teams become more creative in the development of alternative options and solutions to specific problems, issues and concerns. As individual teams become more energized and motivated by an environment of open communication, they tend to become more solution-, action- and results-oriented. A previous emphasis on activity and input is unseated by a motivation to produce results.

Motivation

An empowered team environment characterized by open communication creates a deep sense of motivation within the organization: individuals and teams are more energized to produce results, develop solutions and move the organization forward. Within a fully empowered and open communication environment, teams and individuals see more of a chance for achievement through the efforts of the group and the progress of the organization. Teams and individuals learn to share and celebrate the overall results.

The sense of achievement, motivation and celebration experienced by an empowered group has strong motivational effects and ramifications on the entire organization. Open communication is enhanced, personal motivation increases and the desire of the entire organization to produce results is immediately sensed and measurable. Leaders must learn to foster this sense of celebration and accomplishment, primarily through sustaining open communication in the team environment. Leaders should understand that open and active communication requires ongoing attention; otherwise it is very easy to stumble into the common pitfalls associated with the team communication environment.

POINTS TO PONDER – SOMETHING TO THINK ABOUT

1. What has happened when you have not paid attention to the free-flow of information and open communication within your team environment?
2. What steps have you taken to enhance open communication within your team?

TRAINING ACTIVITY – APPLICATION & ACTION PLAN

1. Within the team environment, identify specific situations that you have observed where the free-flow of information and open communication has had an impact.
    - Information
    - Relationships
    - Conflict
    - Atmosphere
    - Decisions
    - Creativity
    - Motivation
2. For each of the above areas identify how open communication and the free-flow of information has assisted teams in their mission and assignments.
3. Recall the results when open communication was not available in each of these situations.
4. Determine how open communication and the free-flow of information can be enhanced in future situations similar to the ones you have identified.

About the Author

Timothy F. Bednarz, Ph.D. is CEO of the American Management Development Group, Inc. For over 20 years he has researched, designed and authored hundreds of learning and development programs used by Fortune 1000 companies.

He is also the author of *Great! What Makes Leaders Great. What They Did, How They Did It and What You Can Learn from It* (2011).

Speaking Availability

Timothy F. Bednarz, Ph.D. is available for speaking engagements for your next meeting or association event. He can be contacted at 800-654-4935 or by e-mail at timothy.bednarz@majorium.com.

Bulk Sales

Bulk sales of this book or any other titles available from Majorium Business Press. Inquiries can be directed to sales@majorium.com, or by phone at 800-6654-4935.

Quick Order Form

Fax orders: 715-342-1118. Send this form.

Telephone orders: Call 800-654-4935 toll-free. Have your credit card ready.

Email orders: sales@majorium.com

Postal orders: Majorium Business Press, 2025 Main Street, Stevens Point, WI 54481, USA.

Please send the following books:

____

____

____

____

Please send more FREE information on:

❑Catalog ❑Speaking/Seminars ❑Mailing Lists ❑Consulting

Name: ____

Address: ____

City: ______________________ State: _____ Zip: _________

Telephone: ____

Email address: ______________________________________

Sales tax: Please add 5.5% for products shipped to Wisconsin addresses.

Shipping by air:

United States: $4.00 for first book and $2.00 for each additional product.

International: $9.00 for first book; $5.00 for each additional product (estimate).

Made in United States
Cleveland, OH
05 November 2026

47664323R00026